Hope amidst the horror

D1744119

What a bewildering world!
While fish are drinking coffee in Brazil
babies go without milk here...
They feed people with words,
the pigs with choice potatoes.

Nazim Hikmet

Introduction

NEVER HAVE the conflicting priorities of the greed of the rich and the need of the poor stood so starkly exposed.

In the first half of 1991 27 million human beings across the Sahel region and the Horn of Africa faced the slow agony of death by starvation. As aid workers and charities screamed warnings about the urgency of the crisis and struggled to cope on pitiful budgets the US war machine ate up $1 billion a day in its assault on Iraq. The cost of just one Tornado jet, £23 million, would have underwritten the total cost of Save the Children's budget for the Sudan for a whole year. Every ten days the Western powers spend $20 billion on arms. UNICEF estimates that if just $10 were spent on each child per year malnutrition would be halved.

Hunger is endemic to the system in which we live. Each year it kills 18 to 20 million people. Even in a 'normal' year 500 million people in Asia, Latin America and Africa live in what the World Bank defines as 'absolute poverty'. In Africa 100 million out of a population of 530 million do not get enough to eat to stay healthy.

The all too familiar pictures of pot-bellied children give us a mere glimpse of the struggle for survival which is the reality for countless millions of people. Even in the United States 30 million people are now recognised as suffering from real malnutrition.

Why do we live in a world of such twisted logic? What is the connection between the Western powers and the misery of the poor? And what is the solution? Before we answer these questions, let us first look at some of the myths surrounding hunger.

The empty myths:
Is there enough food?

PROBABLY THE most common—and most misplaced—assumption used to explain starvation is that there is not enough food to go round.

For 30 years world food production has on average increased 16 percent faster each year than population size. If we look at cereals alone the picture is one of extreme abundance. Enough grain is grown to make every man, woman and child fat on 3,600 calories a day. The same grain would provide everybody with 6.5 grammes of protein a day.

Nor is it the case that those countries which are the most affected by hunger are unable to produce enough food for domestic production. During the 1970s only 12 percent of the world's population lived in countries where food production per person was falling. In India the re-distribution of less than 6 percent of domestic food production would provide adequate diets for the hungry. In Africa, under 8 percent of Tanzania's food supply and 2.5 percent of that of both Senegal and Sudan would eliminate starvation on the continent.

But in today's world you must either grow your own food or pay for it. The first option has become increasingly difficult in the poorer countries. Land has become concentrated in the hands of fewer and fewer wealthy land owners who ferociously repress attempts to seize back plots by the landless. Competition with Western products such as North American beef or synthetic textiles has encouraged governments to turn more and more of their countries' land over to cash crop production and pasture in order to maintain the value of their exports. Today three quarters of all the privately-held land on the planet is owned by just 2.5 percent of the world's land-owners, with the top 0.2 percent controlling over half.

If growing for self consumption is becoming less of an option, what of paying to eat? And who controls the price?—certainly not the poor!

6

The price of food is precisely regulated by governments and multi-national agricultural conglomerates. The way in which such organisations control prices competes only with the madness of arms competition as an indictment of the system in which we live.

Despite their rhetoric about free trade, both the US and the European powers practice intervention buying of food on a massive scale whenever prices begin to fall to 'undesirable' levels. As one American professor of economics put it:

...if US farm policy over the past half century can be thought of having a theme, it has been to prevent productivity from driving down prices...

In Europe elaborate control mechanisms operate to ensure that food prices stay high. Indeed it is difficult to follow the labyrinthine market regulations of the European Community's Common Agricultural Policy. There are:

deficiency payments—made to farmers if the price of their produce falls;

intervention agencies—through which the Common Agricultural Policy buys up produce for storage if the market is saturated;

abandonment premiums—whereby farmers are paid to take land out of use;

production aid—to encourage farmers to grow certain things rather than others;

export subsidies—to ensure EC produce is competitive on the world market;

subsidies to manufacturers—to ensure that processing companies are not adversely affected by high prices;

denaturing premiums (still operating in the case of sugar)—which have the effect of diverting produce away from human consumption to areas such as the chemical industry;

export taxes—to prevent exports out of the community when CAP prices are lower than world prices. The list is long and tedious.

The end result is that staggering amounts of money are spent every year—not on actually producing, transporting or processing food—but on maintaining the competetive system on which food production is based.

The most powerful symbol of the obscenity of food

production under capitalism must be the food mountains in Europe and North America. Through intervention buying at times of market 'saturation' enormous stocks of produce have been accumulated to be withheld or released in the interest of stable high prices. Between 1982 and 1983—as the Third World reeled under the impact of recession and debt crisis and pot-bellied children appeared on our television screens—stocks of protein-rich milk powder rose from 576,000 tonnes to 916,000 tonnes. By the following year they had tipped over the one million tonne mark. Stocks of butter doubled in the same period from 306,000 tonnes to 622,000 tonnes. Today 200 million tonnes of grain are stored world-wide, 20 million tonnes of which are held by the EC. When the keeping of such stocks first became a 'problem' for the community the logic of the situation was summed up nicely in the Mansholt memorandum of December 1968:

> ...the Community now finds itself saddled, in the case of many products with surpluses of which some cannot even be disposed of on the world market. Even when there are outlets, the surpluses bear on the market so heavily that they can be disposed of only at a price which is very costly to the Community.

The problems of the agricultural community in Europe must have weighed heavily on the minds of the starving of Biafra at that time!

One very effective way of keeping food prices high is not to produce it at all. In the late 1960s and 1970s the US and Canadian governments paid enormous subsidies to their farmers to take land out of production. A secret US government report estimated that this land would jointly have produced over 90 million more tonnes of wheat during 1969-72. In these same years 2 million people perished mainly from starvation and disease in Biafra, as did 500,000 Cambodians and 200,000 in Ethiopia. Between 1968 and 1973 one fifth of the entire Mauritanian population fled the land to escape famine.

As Berthold Brecht put it, 'Famines do not occur, they are organised by the grain trade'.

Deliberate non-investment in rice production, staple to the diet of so many in the underdeveloped world, forced up the price from $129 a tonne in January 1971 to $538 a tonne in April 1974. In the 1980s farmers were paid not to grow potatoes and grain in order to ensure high price stability.

During the Reagan years, whilst hundreds of thousands died in sub-Saharan Africa, the US government contracted the building of grain storage tankers with special hull doors designed to release their contents into the ocean!

It is irrelevant to the food companies exactly how they keep the food off the market—so long as nobody actually eats it and the price remains high. Coffee may be dumped in the ocean off the coast of Brazil, cognac grapes may be converted to industrial alcohol, butter may be allowed to putrify into oil.

Political embarrassment has forced EC officials to allow quantities of food from existing surpluses to be used for emergency relief. At the same time, however, more arable land was to be taken out of production to compensate for any depression in prices.

Destitution in Bangladesh—yet the country has a super-abundance of food

When cheap food is allowed onto the market it is to destabilise the price of produce from the more competitive food exporting countries and to impose market monopolies. Such 'dumping' has meant the complete undercutting of Brazilian sugar exports by subsidised EC sugar. This is despite the fact that Brazil's sugar costs around half that produced in the EC.

Are there too many mouths?

THE OTHER side of the coin to the 'not enough food' position is the idea that there are too many people. This notion originated as a 'scientific' argument with the writings of Thomas Malthus in the nineteenth century.

He claimed population growth would outstrip food production and that the victims of the ravages of early capitalism—the poor who would always be with us—must be

9

left to die. This deeply reactionary argument was used at the time to justify the appalling immiseration of European workers of whom Engels wrote in his **Condition of the Working Class in England** in 1845.

The same argument has risen again in various forms in recent years. In September 1990 a leading article appeared in the respected medical journal, **The Lancet**, written by one Dr Maurice King. In it he argued that babies in the Third World, suffering from dehydration in drought conditions, should not be rehydrated but allowed to die. The article was supported by the journal's editorial. The staggering inhumanity of such an idea, coming as it did from a 'respected' quarter of the medical profession, was matched only by the editorial's choice of imagery. Even if an atom bomb a day were dropped on the Third World, he argued, the pace of population growth would cause social catastrophe by the end of the century.

Far more distressing is the growing influence of such ideas, trimmed of their most overtly violent and racist overtones, on the European and North American left. In Britain for example such leading figures of the Green movement as Jonathan Porritt have called for the abolition of child benefit for the second child to discourage large families.

For such an influential idea it is remarkable just how weak it is. Even when we look at the crude figures this argument as an explanation of world hunger does not hold up. We hear of starvation in India with a population of 247 inhabitants per square kilometre, but not in Holland with 363 per square kilometre. Bolivia, one of the least densely populated countries, with only 7 inhabitants per square kilometre needs no lessons in the meaning of famine.

The picture becomes even clearer if we look at population density in relation to the land available for agricultural use. In Holland only 0.06 hectares are under cultivation per person whereas the figures for Bolivia and India are 0.63 and 0.3 respectively. How is it then that people go hungry in India whereas Holland is a net food exporter?

If we look at the whole of Asia, the most populous continent, those countries which are able to sustain their populations well have the lowest ratios of cropland to population. In China there are 0.13 hectares per person; in

South Korea 0.07; in Taiwan 0.06. Compare these figures to Asian countries where malnutrition is endemic: Pakistan 0.4; Bangladesh 0.16; Indonesia 0.15. Only two generations ago China, with a population of 500 million experienced famine almost every year. Today, with a population of 1,100 million, mass starvation does not occur in that country. *Population size has no relevance whatever in explaining hunger and starvation.*

Despite cries of alarm from many in the Green movement, with only 44 percent of the world's potentially arable land producing food, it has been estimated that the globe could support 10-12 times its present population. Most strikingly, the world's farming area could be increased 50 percent without any serious ecological damage such as deforestation.

Considering the flimsiness of the 'too many mouths to feed' analysis it's astonishing how seriously it has been taken by many Third World governments, and with what force birth control policies have been implemented as a proposed solution to hunger in their countries.

In India the government has suppressed maternity leave for working mothers, paid bounties to doctors for each sterilisation candidate they can haul in, set up mass vasectomy camps and raised the legal marriage age. Over 100,000 people are employed in population reduction work.

In over a dozen countries incentive schemes are used to entice hungry women to undergo sterilisation. In Bangladesh, during the floods of July-October 1984, after the incentives had been increased, the **Bangladesh Observer** noted that sterilisations rose to an unprecedented quarter of a million. Indeed donations of wheat during these months were made conditional on women undergoing sterilisation. Even in their own terms such schemes are a nonsense. If a birth control programme whereby every couple had only two children, were put into effect tomorrow the world's population would not stop growing until well into the next century. More to the point, such thinking fails to understand the real reasons for the high birth rates which *do* exist in some Third World countries.

A popular misconception about large family size amongst the poor is that it is at bottom to do with ignorance and illiteracy. If only there were greater access to contraceptives and information, the argument goes, then the birth rate would start to decline.

The fact is that a poor rural family in Bangladesh will plan their family size every bit as carefully as the most liberally minded couple living in Hampstead. For the poor Bangladeshi couple, children are an economic necessity. By the age of four or five a child provides some labour for the family—fetching water, feeding livestock, taking meals to the fathers and brothers in the fields. By the age of 12 a boy will contribute more than he consumes. Parents know that without children

---

Capitalism's killers

THE TWO most common diseases associated with famine are *kwashiokor* and *marasmus*. Kwashiokor produces the typical pot-bellied syndrome and is caused by protein deficiency. It is also known as 'one-two' disease since it often affects an older child who is weaned off the mother's milk to make way for a new baby. Marasmus produces wizzening and premature ageing in children. It is caused by protein and calorie deficiency.

A host of diseases exploit the reduced resistance that hunger brings. The biggest killers will be *gastro-enteric diseases* and even *measles* which inflicts a mortality rate up to one thousand times higher than in the West.

Those living on a monotonous diet of one or two foods will suffer *vitamin or mineral deficiencies*. 300 million people are affected with *goitre*. Where corn is the only food *pellagra* can bring madness. Where polished rice is the staple diet one in five people suffer *beri-beri*. *Vitamin-A deficiency blindness* affects millions in the Sahel, Indonesia and India.

Babies short of protein and calories in the final intra-uterine weeks and first months of life will suffer permanent brain damage. Cells programmed to multiply in this period fail to do so and the condition becomes irreversible.

12

to look after them in their old age, they will perish. Once we put these considerations alongside the high infant mortality rates it is clear that large family size is a defensive reaction against poverty.

It is poverty that produces high birth rates in the Third World, not the other way around.

What about 'natural' disasters?

ACCOUNTS of disasters which blame the elements—drought, flood or pests—are just as unsatisfactory as those which argue there are too many mouths to feed. When 50,000 old age pensioners die in Britain during a harsh winter we do not simply blame the snow. Instead we ask why they could not pay their heating bills—we look for *social* explanations. The same logic applies in the Third World. Drought is a regular occurrence in the south western United States yet we do not hear of famine there. Drought in the Sahel region of Africa however can cause human tragedy on a massive scale.

Research by the Swedish Red Cross and Earthscan has shown that the annual number of people killed in natural disasters jumped sixfold between the 1960s and 1970s—a far greater jump than either population or the number of disasters. In 1975 **National Geographic** reported satellite pictures of the Sahel during the drought season which showed a hexagonal island of lush pasture in the midst of sunburned scrubland. It was a modern ranch of quarter of a million acres, owned by wealthy land owners or foreign agribusiness. Such farms, which are supported by modern farming infrastructure—irrigation, pesticides and supplemented feedstocks—are well equipped to survive the 'natural' disaster of low rainfall.

Drought of course is nothing new to the inhabitants of the Sahel. But famine on its present scale certainly is. It only began in the era of European capitalist expansion and colonialism. Traditionally the millet granaries of the Sahel region were designed to hold grain for four years and grain was only eaten in the third year of storage. This food reserve buffered the population against the vagaries of climatic change. Only with colonial exploitation and the imposition of taxes did this change. Enforced taxes meant growing cash crops. Growing cash crops meant less land being available for subsistence farming. This in turn meant having to buy food for consumption. Having to buy food meant having to grow more cash crops. This vicious cycle resulted in total depletion of reserves. Thus when drought struck, so too did famine.

Hunger and starvation are the result not of a hostile natural environment but of a hostile social environment. Human beings are no longer slaves to the elements—only to other human beings.

Then as now: the Irish Famine

IF AN event like the great Irish famine of 1845-48 occurred in a Third World country today it would be presented as a human tragedy resulting from natural causes. The combination of a new strain of potato-infecting fungus, *phytopthora infestans*, and damp weather which helped it to spread produced total crop failure.

The 1851 census showed that the population had dropped by two and a half million—from an original eight million. One million had emigrated, many on the plague boats bound for America. One and a half million had perished from hunger and disease.

The human misery of the time was described in 1846 by a Cork magistrate:

'The scenes which presented themselves were such as no tongue or pen can convey the slightest idea of. In the first [hovel], six famished and ghastly skeletons, to all appearances dead, were huddled in a corner on some filthy straw, their sole covering what seemed a ragged horsecloth ... I approached with horror, and found by a low moaning they were alive—they were in fever, four children, a woman and what had once been a man. It is impossible to go through the detail ... in a few minutes I was surrounded by at least 200 such phantoms, such frightful spectres as no words can describe, either from famine or fever. Their demoniac yells are still ringing in my ears, and their horrible images are fixed upon my brain.'

Yet there was nothing 'natural' at all about this catastrophe. Under British colonial rule landlords had the right to impose extortionate rents, evict tenants and tear down their homes. The bulk of peasants' land was of necessity given over to growing grain as a cash crop to pay rent. The only food crop which could be grown in sufficient quantities in the little soil that was left was the potato. Thus millions of peasants became totally dependent on this one crop for their livelihood. When the potato blight struck so did famine. Starving peasants were too physically weak to plant and harvest their cash crop and eviction soon followed. During the abundant wheat harvest of 1847 prices slumped. But this meant nothing to the moneyless, landless peasants at that time.

During the worst years of the famine grain and cattle were actually being exported out of the country. In the three months up to 5 February 1846 258,000 quarters of wheat and 701,000 hundredweight of barley, worth about a million pounds had left Ireland along with 1,000,000 quarters of oats and oatmeal. The head of the British Treasury, Charles Trevelyan, refused to allow grain to be used as relief because it would destabilise the price.

As John Mitchel, the Irish revolutionary put it, 'During all the famine years Ireland was actually producing sufficient food, wool and flax to feed and clothe not nine but eighteen millions of people'. Yet a ship sailing into an Irish port during the famine years with a cargo of grain was 'sure to meet six ships sailing out with a similar cargo'.

Then, as now, hunger did not exist through scarcity but rather in the midst of plenty.

The real roots
of hunger

EVERY COUNTRY today considered part of the Third World has suffered colonial domination and imperialism for a prolonged period of its history. Developing throughout the nineteenth century and reaching its height in the 1890s the colonial expansion of the European powers touched every part of the globe.

Plunder beyond the national boundaries was part and parcel of the development of capitalism in the European countries. Expansion could be achieved either through warfare or through colonialism. Generally speaking the latter was the cheaper and more lucrative. The industrialisation of the late eighteenth and nineteenth centuries shifted huge rural populations into the towns. In the ghetto conditions of the industrial cities of England these workers at least had to be fed—as cheaply as possible. Colonies were needed to supply the commodities which were the stock in trade of the seafaring merchants—tobacco, cotton, cocoa, coffee and sugar. Finally they were necessary to provide the mineral wealth which formed the foundations of the massive capitalist expansion of the twentieth century.

Thus Britain and France, and to some extent Italy, shared out Arabia between themselves. The Spanish already had their colonies in South America. Whole areas of the continent of Africa became British, French, Dutch, Belgian and Portugese possessions. The Europeans wrestled for influence in China. The Indian subcontinent became the jewel in Britain's empire.

Today's world was shaped by the colonialism in the nineteenth century. The pecking order among the top powers has changed and the most direct chains of colonial domination have been thrown off by national liberation movements. Yet still the basic imperialist framework of the world remains intact. The Gulf War showed the Western powers, led by the United States, are still willing to unleash the most ferocious forces of destruction to defend their imperialist interests.

The lower industrial level of the Third World is no accident of history—a matter of time lag or internal deficiency. In a sense it is wrong to think in terms of the developed world *as opposed* to the underdeveloped world. Rather they are two aspects of the same capitalist system.

The development of the poorer countries has been determined by exploitative relations with the dominant world powers into which their national economies have been historically locked. Colonialism has frequently meant the destruction of prosperous economies. The classic example is the destruction of India's thriving textile trade in the early nineteenth century.

When Britain first colonised India in the late eighteenth century its agricultural base was strong, as were its diverse craft industries. Its exports of textiles and metalwork to China, North Africa and Europe totalled £6 million annually. Indian textiles were also undercutting those being produced by British mills. Until 1813 the price of the Indian product was half that of the British. The situation began to change as the British East India Company acquired a monopoly over India's export trade. Artisans were forced to sell at ruinously low prices. At the same time levies of around 70 percent were imposed on Indian imports to Britain. Indian produce became effectively taxed out of the important British market. Meanwhile British goods circulated freely in India. India's manufacturing base was destroyed. The value of India's cotton goods fell from £1,300,000 in 1814 to £100,000 in 1832. As an English Governor-General observed, 'The bones of the weavers were bleaching the plains of India'.

The collapse of the craft industries now had its impact on agriculture. From 1891 to 1931 the population who relied on the land for their subsistence rose from 61 percent to 75 percent. In this mass return to the fields the size of small holdings decreased and the soil became exhausted. Now hunger stalked the country as never before.

On top of these changes the British imposed the *Zemindars*—landlords who collected rural taxes on a commission basis. Under the Permanent Zemindari

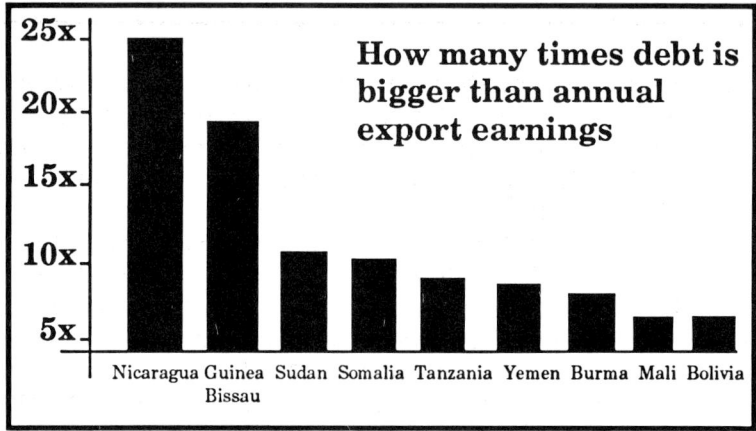

How many times debt is bigger than annual export earnings

Nicaragua Guinea Bissau Sudan Somalia Tanzania Yemen Burma Mali Bolivia

Settlement corruption became rife. Immense power was placed in the hands of these administrators. The Famine Commission of 1880 noted that tenants 'are kept in a situation of absolute dependence on the landlord'. Tenants once again became vulnerable to famine and epidemics as they sold stocks to pay their dues.

A similar story could be told of Bangladesh, today one of the most desperately impoverished countries, yet once the wealthiest part of the Indian sub-continent.

The roots of the present crisis lie in the world recession of the 1970s. The slump in manufacturing worldwide spurred a massive expansion of the money markets. Capital that was no longer being ploughed back into investment was now being speculated on the London and New York markets and credit became available on a massive scale. Third World governments maintained their development programmes by borrowing heavily. But papering over the cracks in this way could not restore stability at the core of the system.

The first straws in the wind of the oncoming crisis came in the late 1970s. The second downward lurch in the long crisis hit hard at Third World trade. Trade deficits for the developing countries doubled from $45 billion in 1979 to $90 billion in 1981. Most of the loans had been borrowed at variable interest rates. As interest rates rose under pressure from US arms spending under Reagan, each increase added billions to debt burdens that were spiralling dangerously out of control. The main creditor banks had loaned far more money than they actually had. By 1985 the nine largest US banks had committed close to $50 billion in loans to Argentina, Brazil, Chile, Columbia, Mexico and Venezuela.

Loans by the big British clearing banks to Latin America stood at £16 billion by the end of 1984. The possibility of a single debtor country defaulting in the opening years of the 1980s sent a shiver down the spine of every banker from Wall Street to the City of London.

The bombshell came in 1982 when Mexico came within a hair's breadth of defaulting on its repayments. Banks had been keen to lend to Mexico during the 1970s to enable the country to develop its oil industry. PEMEX, the Mexican state oil corporation had alone borrowed $20 billion—one quarter of the country's crippling debt. The nine largest US banks had 44 percent of their capital tied up there. The crisis was finally averted through massive intervention by the world financial community, led by the International Monetary Fund. But it had been a close call.

The banks now saw a need to develop a new, tougher perspective on their lending. The IMF imposed conditions before loans could be obtained. Essentially, these were intended to reduce domestic consumption. More specifically they meant cutting back government spending on social services and food subsidies, privatisation of state-run industry and services, abolition of price controls, wage restrictions and higher taxation. Third World governments could not now simply borrow money. Instead they had to subscribe to Structural Adjustment Loans (SALS) and austerity programmes. The consequences were catastrophic.

The example of Jamaica demonstrates graphically how a combination of economic sabotage and IMF-directed restructuring can bring misery to millions. In the 1950s and 1960s the Jamaican economy enjoyed a respectable growth rate of 5-6 percent a year. Trade expanded eightfold in the same period. Compared to other developing countries the infant mortality rate was low, life expectancy high and literacy and health care plans were thriving.

In the 1972 elections Michael Manley's People's National Party swept aside a corrupt and brutal government, promising widespread social reform. The PNP moved to wrest control over the country's main mineral export—bauxite (aluminium ore). A production tax was imposed on the industry. The aluminium conglomerates hit back by moving production out of Jamaica to Africa and Australia.

All of this occurred against a background of declining investment and lower demand for Jamaica's exports. By 1976 Jamaica's foreign currency reserves were zero and Manley turned to the IMF. The conditions were harsh. The fund demanded a $300 million spending cut, equal to 26 percent of the prevous year's budget. 11,000 public sector workers had to be laid off. Disinvestment and capital flight sent unemployment rocketing to 31 percent by 1979. Factories were operating at one third capacity.

The country's debt soared to $1.7 billion in this period. Further austerity measures were demanded, including the loss of 6,200 public sector jobs. Public investment fell by 30 percent. Food subsidies vanished. Real incomes fell by 48 percent between 1983 and 1985.

Jamaica's trade balance had shifted back into surplus by 1984 and the World Bank declared it 'a successful year for

Bolivian tin miner: his fate is decided on the world commodity markets

Jamaica'. The social cost however had been massive and savage. By 1986 an urban family of five needed $J175 a week to maintain an adequate diet. The minimum weekly wage (which in the Third World is close to the average weekly wage) stood at just $J60. Surveys showed that 26 percent of 0-3 year olds in the Kingston area were malnourished. By 1985 the figure had reached 29.5 percent. Another survey showed that 43 percent of mothers were anaemic. In 1982 Jamaica saw its first polio deaths in 30 years. Today, with the country forced to devote over half its export earnings to debt service, the picture does not look set to improve.

Africa provides the most powerful evidence of the profound indifference of a competetive world capitalist system to the real physical needs of human beings. We will look at a few examples.

The debt crisis years have taken a heavy toll indeed on

the population of Zaire. With debts now standing at $8.6 billion, wages have declined 90 percent since the country's independence. 80 percent of the people live in absolute poverty. A year after devaluation of the country's currency was imposed by the IMF in September 1983, an average family in the town of Bakuvu needed 80 Zaires a day for food alone—four times the salary of a semi-skilled worker or a teacher. Malnutrition has been rising since 1983. Cases of kwashiokor have risen dramatically. It is estimated that half the children are now dying before the age of five. In the two biggest cities, Kinshasa and Lubumbashi, the average daily calorie rations are 1,450 and 1,425. According to the Food and Agriculture Organisation the daily calorie intake required for a reasonably active life is 2,300!

Zambia, dependent on copper for 90-95 percent of its foreign exchange earnings has been hard hit by the two thirds fall in the price of copper since 1966. Ordinary Zambians, though not the country's elite, have suffered terribly.

Zambia's debt stands at $820 for each man, woman and child. Its per capita income is just $250. To fully service its debt Zambia would have to devote 195 percent of its export earnings to this alone. The IMF has now stopped all further credit to Zambia. In late 1985 the price of cornmeal, the staple food, shot up 50 percent while bread went up by 100 percent. Fuel prices have doubled.

In Kenya an IMF monitoring official sits in an office in the central bank overseeing government budgetary decisions. IMF policies, plus a slump in the price of tea, have pushed a huge section of the population into absolute impoverishment. By 1982 28 percent of children suffered from stunted growth. In the same year nearly half the children sampled had been sick in the preceeding two weeks.

The scale and urgency of the crisis in Africa is terrifying. It cannot be explained by pointing to any drought. The famines of the early 1990s were entirely predictable—indeed *were* predicted by relief agencies as long ago as 1986.

It is a legacy of the colonial period that the poorer countries export raw materials such as crops and metal ores and import expensive manufactured goods and processed food from the West. This exploitative relationship has been reinforced by the IMF.

The first article of the IMF's charter states as its objective 'To facilitate balanced growth of international trade...[and] seek the elimination of exchange restrictions that hinder world trade'. For the Third World this means that more protective tariffs are broken and that economies become even more locked into a trade system which brings misery to their populations. One of the primary conditions of IMF loans is the increase of exports for the world market.

Yet the value of Third World exports has declined. Fibre optics have replaced copper in the telecoms industry. Plastics have largely replaced sisal and hemp. Man-made fibres have replaced cotton and other natural fibres. Tropical oils no longer compete well with alternatives on the world market.

In April 1987 GATT released figures for Third World trade. The less developed countries held 28 percent of world trade in 1980. By 1986 the figure had dropped to 19 percent. In 1980 the developed countries had drawn 29 percent of their imports from the poorer countries. By 1986 that figure was down to 19 percent. The countries of the Third World, subordinate as many of them are to a single export, are more exposed than they have ever been to the trade winds of the world capitalist market.

The combination of debt and trade crisis has ravaged their economies and has set the scene for the tragedy we see unfolding before us.

Do Western workers benefit?

THERE IS no sense in which workers in the West benefit from the suffering of the poor of the Third World. Indeed 30 million Americans today suffer from hunger. In 1984 a nutritionist testifying before the Texas Senate Interim Committee on Hunger reported treating children with kwashiokor and marasmus. A black infant born today in America's capital city has less chance of survival than one born in Jamaica.
Bosses, with the help of compliant union officials, use the threat of cheap labour in the Third World as an excuse for closing plants in the US and to drive down the wages of US workers.

The hungry do not take their suffering lying down. A world of hunger requires policing. Brutal regimes are maintained at immense cost by the West, along with a constant, world-wide US military presence. In 1988 the US had 333 major bases on foreign soil. The cost of maintaining these bases in 1985 stood at $138 billion—$1,400 in tax for every household in the US. For the same year that compared to $115 going to housing and $126 to education.

But of course there are those who gain enormously from the present system. The food conglomerates— 50 firms make up 75 percent of the industry's profits—have entered the industry simply for the huge profits. Just six multi-national grain corporations handle 90 percent of all the grain shipped in the world.

The profits of these companies come both from cheap, unprocessed food from the Third World *and* from consumers in the West. The US Federal Trade Commission found that in 1972 monopoly power in thirteen industries had cost eaters $21 billion more than they should have paid.

The biggest profits are made by 'adding value' to the crop by processing. In 1974 the US Department of Agriculture stated that 94 percent of the increase in food prices over the previous 20 years was the result of costs added by corporate middle men. In Britain (according to a study by the University of Reading's Centre for Agricultural Strategy) almost half the total spending on food is to cover processing and distribution costs.

Workers in the West positively lose out from the existing system and the oppression in the Third World. It is this that makes solidarity possible. Such identity of interest was shown in 1986 when 350 black workers at a 3M plant near Johannesburg went on strike to protest at the lay off of 172 workers at a sister plant in New Jersey. Such action across the divide between the rich and poor shows a permanent solution to the oppression of Third World poor is not just a pipedream.

The horror:
No solution under capitalism

WESTERN 'AID', coming from the powers which have created the misery in the first place, never has as its aim the ending of suffering. Indeed even the short term emergency relief operations we occasionally see are subordinate to economic, political and strategic interests. As no less a person than Secretary of State George Schultz put it in 1985, 'our foreign assistance programmes are vital to the achievement of our foreign policy goals'.

US foreign aid is only 0.2 percent of its output and total Western aid stands at 0.32 percent of the rich countries' output. This compares with world arms spending of over $800 billion a year. A brief look at the league table of US recipients will show that it is not human need which drives the 'aid' machine.

1. Egypt	**5,444.1**
2. Israel	**5,215.0**
3. El Salvador	**1,286.1**
4. Pakistan	**1,153.7**
5. Turkey	**1,103.5**

(Millions of dollars for fiscal years 1981-1985)

Egypt and Israel alone received fully one third of US aid in this period. On a per capita basis Israel is top of the league, receiving $286 per person. The world's ten poorest countries received less than 5 percent of US assistance in 1985. In Central America three governments regarded as allies—Honduras, El Salvador, and Costa Rica—received $69 per person in that year while the 48 countries of Sub-Saharan Africa got $3 per person.

Only 14 percent of US foreign aid is in the form of food

and only 10 percent of that is for emergency relief. Over half of US food aid is not given away but is sold on credit to loyal and often corrupt governments who are then free to sell it to those who can afford it. Indonesia for example receives $45 million a year in food aid, of which it resells 90 percent.

Three quarters of world aid is 'tied' which means recipients have to spend it on goods produced by the donor country, often at prices above those for the same goods available from other sources. Such 'aid' is in effect a subsidy for the manufacturers of the donor country.

The holders of the US's purse strings are more responsive to requests for aid from co-operative military regimes and those prepared to dance to their tune. Those not prepared to toe the line find that the kind-heartedness of the US wears thin very quickly. US aid to Zimbabwe was cut in half in 1983 after the Zimbabwean government failed to support the US at the United Nations.

Under the reformist government of Salvador Allende in Chile in the early 1970s, US aid was cut to nothing. The US ambassador to Chile declared 'Not a nut or bolt will reach Chile under Allende...we shall do all within our power to condemn Chile and the Chileans to utmost deprivation and poverty'. In the case of Nicaragua economic blockade and the cutting off of food and development aid undermined the popular Sandinista government.

In this, as in other cases, radical Third World regimes have responded to the crisis by turning the screws on their own poor, rather than seeking to spread revolt against the major powers. In the case of the Sandinista regime, this strategy eventually led to its downfall.

Western aid has little to do with feeding people at all. Two thirds of it goes towards military build up and overall budgetary support. Under the Reagan administration military aid became the largest slice of total aid—swelling from 22 percent to 37 percent by 1985. The US has provided $47 billion worth of military equipment to the Third World since the Second World War.

Speaking of the food aid sent to Bangladesh during the 1970s the **Nation** reported that one third of the food went to the military, police and civil service. Another third went to the middle class ration card holders in politically sensitive areas.

The final third, designated for the rural poor, found its way onto the black market. 3,000 deep tube wells from the World Bank went straight to the wealthy land owners who used their extra advantage to push small holders off their land.

The corruption of the regimes sponsored by the West in the Third World means that aid rarely trickles past the ruling elites to those who really need it.

Many of these problems also apply to money collected by charities. However, the motives and aims of donors in this case are quite different. Many of the major charities dealing with international relief originated at times of great human solidarity. The Save the Children Fund for example emerged in 1919 in opposition to the Allied blockade of Germany. Similarly Oxfam was formed to protest against the blockades of the occupied countries after the Second World War. War On Want was inspired by radical ideals in the years immediately following the war and involved many on the Labour left, including the young Harold Wilson.

When millions of ordinary people around the world took part in Sports Aid, for example, there was no strategic interest, no ulterior motive. Contrary to the cynical, pessimistic view according to which we are all motivated by greed, the vast majority of human beings are genuinely horrified at the sight of other human beings in a state of misery.

Popular charity is also different from the philanthropy of the wealthy. The great industrial philanthropists of the nineteenth century, such as George Cadbury, were not doing good for the sake of it. They were concerned above all with the health, efficiency and technical competence of their workforce and also with promoting the work ethic, abstinence, diligence, and industriousness. Neither should we be impressed by the super rich such as Jeffery Archer or Princess Anne managing to forego one slap up lunch in order to save the world.

The problem with charity is by and large not the sincerity of those giving or collecting. It is rather simply the scale of the problem. In 1985 Live Aid raised about $100 million in response to the famine in Ethiopia. Two years later Ethiopia's external debt was over $2,500 million. Debt service was consuming 28.4 percent of the country's output. In 1989 the total debt of the poorest countries in the world stood at $1,113,000 million.

A more fundamental problem with charity as a response to famine is that it deflects our outrage away from the real causes that underlie the horrors. The ability of registered charities to raise the politics of the issue in which they are involved is severely curtailed under the law. In April 1990 Oxfam was forced to drop its support for sanctions against South Africa by the Charity Commissioners. When Oxfam, publicly called in 1990 on the British government to do something which could genuinely begin to solve the problem of famine in Africa—abolish the affected countries' debt to Britain—they were taken to task and threatened with court action for being 'too political'. In fact most charities do not go even this far.

Not to talk about the real causes of hunger in the world—the banks, the IMF, the market, imperialism—leaves us scratching at the surface, dealing only with symptoms.

Famine and starvation are not unfortunate accidents of our times. They are the absolutely necessary products of a system which puts the price of fo above feeding the hungry—which puts profits before need. The food is there—in abundance. But whether it reaches the mouths of those who need it lies in the hands of capitalists and bureaucrats.

Ultimately the problem is one of power. To put an end to the horror of famine we must look to a social force which has the potential to destroy the real source of the problem.

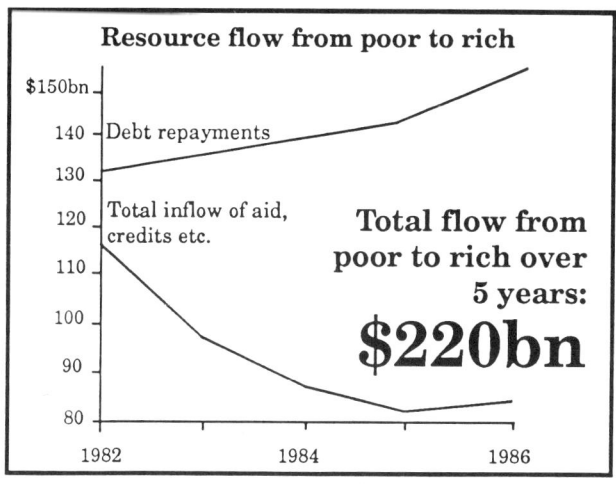

Resource flow from poor to rich

$150bn
140 — Debt repayments
130
120 — Total inflow of aid, credits etc.
110
100
90
80

1982   1984   1986

Total flow from poor to rich over 5 years:

$220bn

The hope:
Socialism and the fight to feed the world

CONTRARY TO the media image of the hungry as being utterly passive, uncomprehending victims of circumstances beyond their control, the hungry *do* fight against their situation and often *do* understand the reason for their plight. During the great Irish famine riots took place in the port towns to prevent the export of grain to England. Riots broke out in Jamaica when the price of kerosene rose in 1985. People danced around barricades to a tune called 'Capitalism Gone Mad'—a popular calypso number of the time.

Despite these revolts, and many others like them, however, the system which perpetuates the misery we observe in the Third World remains. To destroy it we must look to a class which because of its cohesion and location in society has the potential to strike at the heart of that system. This exists today in the form of the industrial working class and much of what is called the service working class.

Workers are impelled to act collectively. Whereas a peasant can own his or her livestock, plough or plot of land, the worker cannot take home his or her bit of train, mine, or factory. From such circumstances a growth of collective consciousness is possible and out of this a coherent alternative to the present system based on the socialisation of production through workers' control—a socialist alternative. Also, workers are organised by capitalism at the point where the production of wealth takes place. This gives them a power and a centrality to society which other social groups do not have. At the same time workers are exploited by capitalism, in both the rich and the poor countries. They have no stake in capitalism. Their interests lie in the overthrow of the system that oppresses them. In 1917 in Russia, against a background of starvation and war, workers led a revolution which did precisely that.

28

The 1917 revolution involved the setting up of workers' councils to organise the distribution of food and the allocation of resources according to need rather than profit. Workers ran their own factories and peasants seized their landlords' land. At this time the working class made up less than 7 percent of the total population. Yet the social weight the working class carried made the revolution possible.

So what is the situation in the Third World today?

The most important trend in Third World societies over the last half century has been the population shift away from the land into the cities. Indeed nine of the world's largest cities are now in the Third World. The following table gives some indication of the scale and momentum of this shift, giving urban population as a percentage of the total.

	1988	2000 (est)
Somalia	35%	44%
Zaire	38%	46%
Angola	27%	36%
Libya	68%	76%
Nigeria	34%	43%
Brazil	75%	83%
Indonesia	27%	36%
Ethiopia	12%	17%
Bolivia	50%	58%
Philippines	41%	49%

In 1985 one quarter (680 million) of Asia's 2.8 billion people were living in cities. By 2000 the figure will have reached 1.4 billion.

These cities have grown on top of industries and, with the development of capitalism in the Third World we have also seen the growth and development of its working class. This has proceeded apace even in those countries most crushed by imperialism. In Zambia, for example, the industrial and service working class together accounts for over 60 percent of the economically active population.

There are more industrial workers in South Korea today than there were in the world when Marx and Engels wrote the **Communist Manifesto**. And the working class of the

Third World is increasingly conscious of its strength and importance. There is hardly a country in the developing world today in which there is not a significant level of trade union organisation. The emergent workers' movements of Africa have flexed their muscles and felt the strength they possess. In 1990/91 workers played a key role in bringing down repressive regimes in a chain of revolts which flashed across the continent. The mighty black working class of South Africa which may yet become the pivot of the African revolution has shaken the brutal apartheid regime to its foundations.

The workers of the Third World will liberate themselves and the oppressed of their countries. Their revolutions will have as their aims the immediate seizure of control over food, the annulment of all foreign debt, the redistribution of land to the peasants and workers' control of production.

For us in the West the primary responsibility to the starving of the world lies in the struggle of ideas to convince workers here that their interests are the same as those of the workers and oppressed of the Third World.

All our futures, both as workers and as human beings lie in solidarity with the Asian, African and Latin American working class in the struggle for a socialist world.

Revolution in the Philippines—even the most repressive regimes have been shaken by uprisings

Suggested further reading

Susan George's **How the Other Half Dies** remains a classic, if slightly dated introduction to the politics of world food production. Her more recent book **A Fate Worse than Debt** offers a definitive analysis of the consequences of debt in the Third World.

Again slightly out of date, but an excellent read, is Nigel Harris's account, **Why Half the World Goes Hungry**. For an account of the arguments surrounding population growth, read **Environment in Crisis, the Socialist Answer**, by Duncan Blackie.

Despite being slightly influenced by Maoist ideas **World Hunger: 12 Myths** by Lappe and Collins takes many of the arguments about hunger head on. Also useful is Sue Buchanan's **Food, Poverty and Power**.

For a more historical and academic treatment see David Arnold's **Famine**. For a really comprehensive summary of facts and statistics see **Third World Guide 90/91** published by Institiuto del Tercer Mundo.

For further reading on imperialism and the politics of Third World leaders, the most up to date accounts are both to be found in the quarterly journal **International Socialism**. See, for instance 'Marxism and Imperialism Today' (**IS 50**) and 'Imperialism, Capitalism and the Third World' (**IS 35**) both by Alex Callinicos.

HOPE AMIDST
THE HORROR

Women at the head of the Turkish miners demonstration.
In November 1990, 48,000 miners in Zonguldak,Turkey began an eight week strike for more pay. Their struggle rapidly broadened, people from the community and other workers joined in. The strike did not stay limited to wages, it took up political demands, for 'bread, peace and democracy'

THE SOCIALIST ANSWER TO WORLD HUNGER

Are there really too many mouths to feed? Are droughts really to blame for the disasters in Africa?

Our planet bulges with food, yet millions face starvation. Hundreds of millions suffer for lack of a basic diet. Governments devote budgets and armies to keeping granaries locked to the hungry.

At the end of the twentieth century starvation is not natural. It is not even an accidental blemish on an otherwise smooth-running system. Capitalism doesn't work other than by denying its products to the needy.

Millions of ordinary people in the West want to end this obscenity.They give gladly to any appeal which promises to help. Yet this trickle of comfort is drained a thousand times over by repayments on Third World debt.

Socialism would be too complex in the modern world, say our critics. Yet there could be nothing more simple than feeding the hungry. No obstacle stands in the way other than capitalism itself

ISBN 0905 998 790

9 780905 998794

ISBN 0 905 998 79 0
£1.20